D0290762

HERMIT CRABS

KW-098

CONTENTS

Photography:
All photos by Judy Ronay except as follows and as noted in captions: Dr.
Herbert R. Axelrod: Cover, 5, 31, 42 (bottom), 52, 74 (bottom), 83, 91;
Paul Bartley: endpapers, 26, 59; Darling Pet Farms: 69; Mervin F. Roberts:
48, 49, 56, 63, 76, 93; Takemura & Suzuki: 18, 19.

Special thanks to Robin Rosenthal, who served as model for a number of
the photos in this book (pages 12, 26-27, 30, 35, 38-39, 43, 44-45, 89) and to
Tropaquarium (Oakhurst, NJ) for providing supplies and information.

Distributed in the U.S. by T.F.H. Publications, Inc., 211 West Sylvania
Avenue, PO Box 427, Neptune, NJ 07753; in England by T.F.H. (Gt. Britain)
Ltd., 13 Nutley Lane, Reigate, Surrey; in Canada to the pet trade by Rolf C.
Hagen Ltd., 3225 Sartelon Street, Montreal 382, Quebec; in Southeast Asia
by Y.W. Ong, 9 Lorong 36 Geylang, Singapore 14; in Australia and the South
Pacific by Pet Imports Pty. Ltd., P.O. Box 149, Brookvale 2100, N.S.W.
Australia; in South Africa by Valid Agencies, P.O. Box 51901, Randburg 2125
South Africa. Published by T.F.H. Publications, Inc., Ltd, the British Crown
Colony of Hong Kong.

NEAL PRONEK

HERMIT CRABS

The two small hermit crabs above represent a new hobby, that of keeping these interesting creatures in your home. Yes, it's very possible . . . and not too difficult.

Introduction

Take a close look. Isn't this an interesting animal? After you have studied the photography for a while, close your eyes and try to remember how many legs it has!

Within the last few years the keeping of land hermit crabs as pets has become more popular than it ever has been before. This wasn't very hard to do, because land hermit crabs never were very popular before. As a matter of fact, they were decidedly unpopular. That is, nobody kept them.

But that's all behind us now. Right now land hermit crabs are hot as pets. They don't get the money spent on them that dogs and cats and tropical fish do, and they don't get the publicity that really oddball pets like tarantulas do, and they haven't even yet become identified as "pets" the way ham-

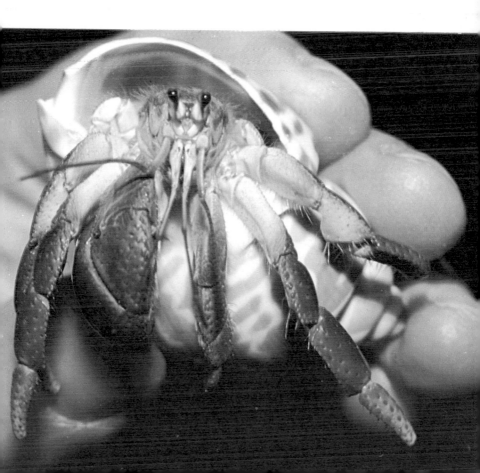

sters, guinea pigs and gerbils have, but they've still carved out a niche for themselves. They're not really big yet, but they're on the way up.

There are reasons for this. Land hermit crabs offer many advantages as pets. They're inexpensive, they don't make a mess (and smell) the way some pets do, they're hardy and interesting, and they're small. Their main disadvantage as far as being kept as pets is concerned is that they don't respond to affection. They are not, in other words, cuddly. They can be considered attractive (depending on how your tastes run) and can be highly colorful (depending mainly on the shells you provide for them), but they're not cuddly and pettable. Many people, in fact, say they're ugly and repulsive, which must be pretty close to the opposite of cuddly and pettable.

Land hermit crabs didn't start to get a big play in the pet trade until well after the decline of baby turtles as pets. The turtles, once a staple livestock item offered in pet shops throughout the country, fell out of favor as pets because their sale was proscribed in many places after it was discovered that under certain conditions they can transmit diseases to people. The disease most often mentioned in connection with baby turtles was salmonellosis, a digestive disorder caused by bacilli of the genus *Salmonella*. The disease is transmitted by about nine million other things besides baby turtles, but most of those things (chicken eggs, for example) are economically much more important than baby turtles. They were therefore left alone while baby turtles took the rap.

Within a few years after the baby turtle flap started it became very difficult to obtain a baby turtle as a pet; in some places it became impossible to obtain one legally. Still, people wanted a pet similar to baby turtles in general characteristics—interesting, small, cheap, and supposedly easy to house and keep. Land hermit crabs seem to fit the bill very nicely, and that's the single biggest reason for their current popularity. They've taken the place of the once-ubiquitous baby turtle in the pet field. People who once would have bought a baby turtle or two now buy a land hermit crab or two. This turtle-replacement business *probably* also is the reason behind the sudden rise in popularity of such unlikely candidates for pet status as tarantulas and scorpions, but of course we can't be sure—any more than we can really be sure that land hermit crabs have become popular only because baby turtles disappeared from the market.

It happens that land hermit crabs are very much superior to baby turtles as pets in a number of important considerations. In the first place, it's easier to provide what they need. Baby turtles are not truly that easy to keep if you're going to pay any real attention to their needs, which is probably why they died off as quickly as they did once they got into the hands of a not-very-knowledgeable owner, often a small child. In the second place, land hermit crabs are a lot less messy than baby turtles, so doing the housekeeping for them is much easier.

In any event, land hermit crabs make good pets for people who want to keep, for themselves or their children, a captive animal of some sort but don't want to knock themselves out taking care of it and don't want to invest much money in purchasing it or housing it. If that's why you've already bought or are about to buy a land hermit crab or a couple of land hermit crabs, you've made a wise choice.

Don't get the idea, though, that land hermit crabs let you home free as far as providing the proper care is concerned. They don't need much, but they have certain requirements that have to be met. They're not very much like us in looks or biology or degree of intelligence, so we have a natural tendency to downgrade their worth in the scheme of things. But that doesn't mean that we're free to inflict unnecessary suffering on them. They're lowlife, all right, but they're alive, and no doubt in their own dimwitted way they're able to experience some of the pains that we ourselves can feel. Assuming that we're responsible for the animals we master,

Your land hermit crab hobby will soon become a shell collecting hobby too. The hermit crabs will outgrow their shells and require larger ones. These larger shells must always be available to the crabs since they won't give you any notice of their outgrowing their old homes.

We owe it to our crabs to provide their necessities and to protect them—from cats, for example. **Opposite:** Freshly cleaned gravel being added to aquarium.

we owe it to our crabs to give them what they need. And if we discover—either before or after we begin to keep them—that we're not willing or able to meet their requirements, we shouldn't keep them at all. They're not toys, and they're not ours to torture through ignorance or neglect or downright cruelty.

We also owe something to ourselves in the keeping of land hermit crabs. We owe it to ourselves to learn something about them—about their biology, about where they come from and how they fit into what we perceive to be the big picture of animal relationships, how they get along in the wild. Fortunately, what we're willing to learn about land hermit crabs on a purely speculative basis can be put to good use in providing the crabs with good care. It's my purpose here to tell you not only how to care for your crabs but also why they need the things they do—because if you know why, you'll probably be much better disposed to give them an even break in the form of good care. In which case both you and your pets will be better off.

Land
Hermit
Crabs
in General

In the upper photo are two marine crabs. They are NOT hermit crabs, but they illustrate how nasty crabs can be. The light-colored crab is about to cut off the eye of the larger crab! The hermit crab shown to the right would merely pull himself inside the shell he carries around if any danger manifests itself.

Land hermit crabs are arthropods. But so are ants and bees and fleas, and so are spiders and centipedes and millipedes and horseshoe crabs. Now obviously there is a big difference between a land hermit crab and a bee. For one thing, bees have wings and hermit crabs don't. For another, bees make much better symbols, getting their name and picture into and onto promotions for businesses of all sorts, mostly as a consequence of their reputation for hard work and productivity, whereas you never hear of Land Hermit Crab Tuna Fish. Therefore, saying that they're both arthropods really doesn't tell us much about either of them. Unfortunately, in order for it to tell us much we're going to have to start getting involved in some basic taxonomy, which means that

we'll have to throw around some words that most people—you possibly among them—don't want anything to do with. But stick with it; at the level at which we're operating, taxonomy is simple memory work, because all we'll be doing is parroting what people who take taxonomy very seriously have said over the course of time. Personally I've never been able to understand why a person—an automobile mechanic, let's say—who has faced and mastered a barrage of automotive terms and concepts much more complicated than any terms and concepts required to give him an understanding of basic taxonomic workings, should feel unwilling or unable to get involved with basic taxonomic considerations as they apply to the animals he's interested in. The taxonomic words are usually longer and foreign-sounding and harder to pronounce, but they serve exactly the same function as the names of tools and automobile parts: they categorize things by giving them different names according to their different appearances and functions and relationships. There is no essential difference between learning to recognize the differences between wrenches and screwdrivers (and then breaking wrenches and screwdrivers into subcategories) and recognizing the differences between arthropods and vertebrates (and then breaking the arthropods and vertebrates into different subcategories). All it takes is a little familiarity with the nomenclature and a desire to use that nomenclature correctly. You can brush up on the nomenclature right here, and I'm going to assume that if you've read this far you already have the desire, so let's get to it.

CLASSIFICATION OF LAND HERMIT CRABS

Land hermit crabs are members of the animal kingdom, Animalia. They, like you and yours and everything else mortal that isn't a plant or a mineral or some indefinable semisomething, are animals. The animal kingdom is divided into a number of less all-embracing groups, called phyla; the group to which the land hermit crabs belong is called the phylum Arthropoda—the phylum that contains all invertebrate bilaterally symmetrical animals having bodies segmented into different-looking areas and covered by a relatively hard body wall that they shed and renew from time to time and onto which are attached jointed legs. The phylum of arthropods is divided into two subphyla, the Mandibulata and the Chelicerata, each of which is further subdivided into a number of classes. One major structural difference between the two subphyla is that the mandibulate animals have antennae and the chelicerate animals don't. The difference isn't always obvious—some mandibulates have very small and hardly noticeable antennae, whereas some of the chelicerates have appendages that very definitely appear to be antennae—but it's always there.

Land hermit crabs have antennae, so they're placed in the subphylum Mandibulata, along with millipedes (class Diplopoda), insects (class Insecta), centipedes (class Chilopoda) and two other classes, both containing worthless little hooples that nobody cares about. The subphylum Chelicerata, by the way, includes the horseshoe crabs (class Xiphosura) and the spiders and scorpions (class Arachnida), plus a few classes of less beloved creatures, so you can see that within the last few years the American pet-keeping public, for whom tarantulas and land hermit crabs have become big stuff, has embarked on an arthropod lovefest. Maybe within a few more years we'll start paying attention to some of the home-entertainment stars of the phylum Annelida by getting leech-happy as well.

Okay, now we have the land hermit crabs pinned down as to their phylum and subphylum, so we'll proceed to the next less inclusive taxon, the class. Land hermit crabs are in the class Crustacea. Crustaceans are distinguished from other members of the subphylum Mandibulata by the possession of two pairs of antennae instead of only one. There are other differences, of course, some of them more immediately ob-

Crabs come in many bizarre shapes and sizes. This one is sometimes called a "spider crab". They do well in marine aquariums. This species is known as *Latreillia phalangium*.

vious than the number of antennae, but that one characteristic immediately separates the crustaceans from crustaceany-looking insects and separates insecty-looking crustaceans (sowbugs, for instance) from insects.

The class Crustacea is subdivided into numerous different orders; the order that contains the land hermit crabs is the order Decapoda, which word literally means "ten-footed." This order contains all of the crustaceans that are worth talking about, the lobsters and crabs and shrimps. Some of the most important anatomical characteristics that land hermit crabs share in common with other decapods are that in these animals a shield-like hard apparatus called the carapace covers the entire head and thorax region (cephalothorax) and that the first (closest to the head) pair of legs end in claws. (This last-named point is not true of *all* decapods, but it's true of by far the most of them, including the land hermit crabs.)

The order Decapoda is broken down into a large number of different families, with the animals we know in general as crabs and lobsters and shrimps each forming a number of families of their own. The land hermit crabs are in the family Coenobitidae, the family that contains the famous coconut crab (also called robber crab), *Birgus latro,* an animal that is agile enough and well armed enough and persistent enough supposedly to climb a coconut tree, knock coconuts off the tree and then proceed to tear through both husk and shell to get to the coconut meat.

The family Coenobitidae contains more than one genus, but the only land hermit crabs that most owners will ever see belong to the genus *Coenobita.* The most commonly seen (in pet shops at least) species in the genus is *Coenobita clypeatus,* a crab that ranges from the Florida Keys southward through the Caribbean area to Venezuela, occurring on both the mainland and Caribbean islands.

Incidentally, land hermit crabs are not the only crabs that can live on land for long periods of time. There are some regular (that is, non-hermit type) crabs that are just as much at home in a purely terrestrial setting as hermit crabs are. Also, not all crabs that live in water necessarily live in salt water; some live in freshwater habitats like lakes and streams.

PHYSIOLOGICAL CHARACTERISTICS

Certain features of land hermit crab physiology must be paid attention to if you're going to keep the crabs successfully. They affect the crabs' capacity to live in the environment you provide, so you have to give them some weight. I'd say that the most important physiological/behavioral characteristics of land hermit crabs as far as keeping them is concerned are:

1.) Land hermit crabs must be provided with shells into which they can stick their abdomens. Land hermit crabs without shells are unhappy land hermit crabs, and pretty soon they're dead land hermit crabs. They *must* be provided with shells or, in addition to the purely physical debilities and dangers that a shell-less condition will induce, they'll start having nervous breakdowns. Now you might think I'm kidding about this, but that's the best way I can think of to describe the behavior of a land hermit crab deprived of its shell for any protracted period: it has a nervous breakdown. It gets purely frantic. Really, land hermit crabs' attachment to and fascination with shells is continuous; they want those shells, and they'll do everything in their power to make sure that they don't get cut off from them. Pinch, scratch, smash, kill—whatever, they'll do it to hang onto (or obtain) a suitable shell.

Considering that it certainly isn't going to cost you much to provide enough shells to keep a whole army of land hermit crabs happy or at least reasonably stable and that observing their shell mania provides you with one of your greatest pleasures of owning land hermit crabs in the first place, you shouldn't stint on shells. Give the crabs shells of all sorts and let the crabs mess around with them to their hearts' content.

There are hundreds of species of crabs. The beautiful marine crab shown to the right is almost perfectly camouflaged. Photo by Keith Gillett. The two *Dardanus* species shown above and below are marine hermit crabs. Photos by Roger Steene.

2.) Land hermit crabs grow, and as they grow they require larger shells. The crabs don't grow the way we do, at a more or less continuous rate. They grow instead in discrete steps. Like all other arthropods, land hermit crabs have at least one part of the body covered by a hard shield. Naturally this hard shield (called the carapace), which in land hermit crabs covers the entire head and thorax region (the cephalothorax), is not elastic, so in order for a land hermit crab to put on size it has to periodically burst out of its old carapace and get into a new and larger one. This it does by molting. The old carapace splits open, and the crab emerges from the old suit of armor. At this stage the crab is relatively soft all over, not on just its abdomen, but it soon hardens up. Freshly molted crabs of course need larger shells if they're not going to be badly cramped, so that's another reason for providing a good variety of shells for your crabs.

3.) Land hermit crabs can climb. The shells that they wear may be clumsy and comparatively heavy, but land hermit crabs' other equipment stands them in good stead in the climbing department. They're no Hillarys, but they get there. Their first pair of legs, being as they are a fairly efficient set of grasping claws, enable the crabs to hang onto and pull themselves toward convenient projections on the surfaces they're climbing, and the second two pairs of legs, ending as they do in sharp points, are great for wedging and bracing; these legs are used by climbing crabs much the same way as a mountain climber uses his pitons. The fourth and fifth pairs of legs are always kept encased within the shell and therefore aren't used during climbing at all—but the other three pairs get the job done. Therefore you have to treat pet land hermit crabs as potential escape artists, and you can't provide them with easy avenues along which to climb and crawl their way to freedom. Remember that land hermit crabs are also known as treecrabs.

4.) Land hermit crabs can regenerate lost legs and eyes and antennae. The lost appendages reappear at the molt that succeeds the loss. They'll reappear, that is, if the molt isn't too close in time to the loss of the appendage(s) involved. Don't expect an about-to-molt crab that loses a leg on Tuesday to pop up with a new one after a molt on Wednesday. And don't expect a crab that has an extraordinary amount of regenerating to do (one claw and two legs, say) to do it all in one molt. Also, don't expect the regenerated appendage(s) to be always the equal in size and strength of the lost one(s); unless the appendage being replaced was lost only shortly after the last molt, its replacement won't be of full size. And don't expect your crabs to molt at all unless you provide them with the proper conditions, the proper conditions in this case being moisture and a sheltering material into which they can dig and feel safe until their freshly assumed (and therefore softer and less protective) exoskeleton hardens up.

5.) Land hermit crabs have gills. Actually, the gills of land hermit crabs are so close to lungs as efficient absorbers of oxygen directly from the air that the crabs' breathing apparatus could almost qualify as lungs instead of gills, but they still require the one thing that gills have to have in order to function: they must be kept moist. A land hermit crab's gills don't have to be immersed in water to work, the way a fish's do, but they have to be kept moist. At the very least, they have to be protected from desiccation.

6.) Land hermit crabs are lovers of warmth. They come from tropical and semitropical areas, and their best temperature range is from 75 to 80° F. Below 75° they start to slow down a little; below 70° they slow down a lot.

All of the points mentioned above are important because they deal with what the crab will do and what you should do. They and their effects will be covered in following sections when we get down to exploring the day-to-day routine involved with keeping the crabs. For now, just keep them in mind, because they'll be handy in helping to understand the reasons *why* specific recommendations are made about keeping the crabs.

Before you go out to your local pet-shop and buy any hermit crabs, like the one shown above, you should learn something about their needs. The tropical aquarium is ideal for a home. Decorate the tank a bit (right). You can even use the same gravel you had in your fish tank!

Selecting Your Equipment

Before you buy a land hermit crab or a group of land hermit crabs you should consider what you can offer them by way of an environment comfortable for them to live in and comfortable for you to provide. Somewhere between the one extreme of building a tropical paradise to house your crabs and the other of stuffing them into a pint milk container lies the correct approach for them and for you: something you both can live with without having either you or the crabs suffer noticeably.

There is just no point in your making more of a cash outlay than you can afford to provide room and board for pet land hermit crabs. If you injudiciously spring for a super-jazzbo layout during your first flush of enthusiasm—during the time, that is, when you might look upon the ownership of crabs as the fulfillment of your yearnings for entertainment and biological knowledge and companionship and

whatever else you think you'll get from the crabs—and then get tired of the crabs in a hurry, you'll be stuck with a lot of highly specialized and therefore generally useless paraphernalia. And you'll almost certainly grow to blame the crabs for your predicament, in which case you might take to bashing them off the walls. That would be bad on two counts:

1. It's not the crabs' fault, so it's not fair.
2. It might lead to additional expense.

There is no sense, either, though, in buying crabs and hoping to save money on your total investment by trying to press a bundle of ill-suited junk into service for housing them. That's a self-defeating enterprise, and you'll simply end up by quickly losing the investment you made in the crabs. Shoeboxes and pots and pans and cut-down bleach containers might make fine temporary housing quarters, but for long-term living they're out.

The middle ground, the sensible ground in this case, is to buy the right type of equipment but to start on a small scale. That will enable you to enjoy your crabs the way they're supposed to be enjoyed (with them healthy and you interested) long enough for you to make up your mind about whether you'd like to expand your crab-keeping activities, keep them at the same level or abandon them entirely.

My recommendation for starting up in the crab game boils down to this: get good stuff, but don't get much of it. If you start small you start smart.

HOUSING

In my view, the unqualifiedly all-around best housing unit for land hermit crabs is the standard tropical fish tank. A tropical fish tank, now, not a goldfish bowl. (Although, come to think of it, a goldfish bowl probably is better suited for keeping a land hermit crab than for keeping a goldfish.) Tropical fish tanks offer many advantages. They offer distortion-free viewing, relative ease of cleaning, portability and the capacity for being lighted and covered easily. Additionally, they have the handy feature of being easily vertically partitioned and horizontally compartmented; you can break the tank up into "rooms," and you can create discrete areas on the bottom.

A 5-gallon or 10-gallon tank would be a good size for a beginning land hermit crab setup. The 10-gallon tank of course offers more room and will accommodate more crabs, and since it's not twice as expensive as a 5-gallon tank it offers a better all-around buy, so probably it's your best bet if you have the room to fit it into the spot in your home in which you plan to place the crab tank.

Fish tanks manufactured today are almost invariably of the all-glass variety; they're made of five slabs of glass butted together with silicone cement and (often) banded at the edges with plastic. Such tanks are much lighter than the old slate-bottomed metal-framed aquariums, so they're less clumsy to maneuver. They're also less expensive. One big advantage that you as a crab-keeper have over a fish-keeper is that the fish tank you use doesn't have to be watertight, so you can make use of the "leakers" that are occasionally returned to pet shops as defective; leakers can be bought at a big discount when you can find them.

Some people don't like the severely cubical look of fish tanks, however, preferring what they consider to be the more graceful lines of the standard "turtle bowl"—the one-piece short, broad, gently curved glass bowl still carried by many pet shops as catch-all containers for small non-mammalian pets of all types. If you eschew the fish tank for any reason, get a bowl of the configuration described; don't get a high, slab-sided (or, worse yet, spherical) goldfish bowl.

COVERS

Keeping a tight-fitting cover on your crab tank will help to keep the crabs in and potential enemies out. If the cover is effective as a vapor barrier between the atmosphere in the tank

The unqualifiedly best housing unit for land hermit crabs is the standard tropical fish tank. Not only because you get a lot for your money since they are mass produced, but petshops usually sell them at very low prices to encourage children to begin with aquariums as their hobby. Often (facing page) your dealer will have an old "leaker" which you might even be able to buy cheaper than normal.

and the atmosphere in the room around the tank it also will help to retard evaporation. Retarding evaporation is important for two reasons. For one thing, you don't want your crab tank's atmosphere to become too dry; although the crabs' respiratory mechanisms are far removed from the type of gills (a fish's, for instance) that can function only when completely immersed in water, a land crab's gills definitely do function more efficiently in a moist atmosphere. If they were not periodically moistened and were allowed to dry out completely, the crab would eventually suffocate. Now that's not to say that you have to keep your crabs in a miniature steambath or create for them a perpetual aqueous miasma. In the wild crabs often take up residence miles away from the ocean, in relatively dry areas, so they're not fog-bathed all the time. They need to keep their gills from drying out, but they don't have to keep them saturated.

Another reason for wanting to retard evaporation is that evaporation is a cooling process, and you want to keep the crabs warm. A solid cover will slow up evaporation and will help to retain heat in the tank if a source of heat is positioned in the tank itself.

The most effective covers for crab tanks are the same as the ones that are most effective for a fish tank: full-hood reflectors and hinged glass tops. Since both types are normally used in conjunction with lighting equipment, we'll discuss them as part of that topic.

LIGHTING EQUIPMENT

Lighting equipment for an individual fish tank—and therefore for a crab home made from a fish tank—almost always consists of what aquarium hobbyists call a "reflector," a bulb-holding unit that sits on top of the tank and shines light down into it. There are two basic types of aquarium reflectors: strip reflectors and full hoods. A strip reflector spans the tank the long way but covers only part of the tank; to cover the entire top, a piece of material (glass is almost always used, although some other materials are suitable) has to be used with the strip reflector to cover the open area not covered by the strip reflector. Full hoods cover the entire top of the tank; they're hinged to allow access to the tank without removing the hood. They also have small scalloped cutouts to allow heaters to be hung on the rim of the tank; you won't be using a heater in the same way an aquarist uses a heater, so you'll be better off covering up the cut-out sections.

Most reflectors sold these days hold fluorescent rather than incandescent bulbs, but incandescent reflectors can be obtained. Incandescent bulbs throw off much more heat than fluorescent bulbs and therefore can be better as providers of heat for the crab tank, but if you use too large a wattage factor you can make things too hot. Additionally, the fluorescent reflectors are more amenable to being equipped with bulbs that give a more subdued and less harsh light. Because the crabs are basically dusk and nighttime animals that in the wild don't do much wandering around in bright daylight, the quality of light given them can be important. They should not be made to feel uncomfortable under a glare.

HEATING EQUIPMENT

Your lighting system, as noted, can play an important part in heating your crabs' home. In fact, apart from the heat derived from the room in which the crabs' tank is situated, the lighting system might provide the only ongoing source of heat. This is because it simply is not esthetically pleasing or economical to heat the crab tank by using the same means by which a fish tank is usually heated. You can do it, but it forces you into doing a lot of complicated contriving, and even then you can end up with a hodgepodge setup.

A thermostatically controlled hanging (that is, partially submerged) aquarium heater can be hung on the side of a water-filled jar deep enough to take the heater. The heater will heat the water, which will in turn throw off heat into the

If you are wise enough to use a standard aquarium for the care and housing of your hermit crabs, you can manage to get all of the rest of your equipment from the same petshop. An aquarium background, gravel, ornaments, reflectors for the top of the tank, and a heater of some sort. Read the section on HEATING EQUIPMENT which starts on page 33 to get some idea of what you are in for as far as heating is concerned.

tank. This method can be effective, but it's not very good-looking, and it's not easy to hide. The other major type of aquarium heater, the completely submergible heater, can be used in the same way as the hanging type and also can be used to heat a small enclosed pool of water in the crab home—more or less a tank within a tank. This system makes it possible to hide the heater much more artfully than is possible with the hanging heater. Unfortunately, completely submergible heaters are much more expensive than hanging heaters. Also, you might not want to use the submergible heater system if you have any really large crabs in the tank, because at least part of the power cord would have to be accessible to the crabs. If a large crab were to nip through enough of the cord's insulation to expose some of the wiring, you'd have a potentially dangerous situation on your hands.

The length of time a heater would have to be working in order to do its job of heating the crab tank would depend partly on the size of the tank and partly on the power of the heater, but of course the biggest factor would be the difference between the desired temperature in the tank and the temperature of the room housing the tank. If the room gets overly chilly and you're trying to maintain a temperature of around 75 degrees in the tank, the heater will be working practically continuously—and it's going to run up your electric bill on you. Therefore it makes sense to situate the crab tank in a room that doesn't get too cold; keep it out of unheated sunporches and places like that, and keep it out of drafts.

If you're concerned about the amount of electric power you might have to consume to generate enough heat to keep your crabs comfortable, there is one relatively inexpensive thing you can do to help cut down your electric bill: insulate the tank. Insulation placed on three sides and the bottom of the tank will reduce heat loss considerably and still allow viewing the crabs by leaving one side unobstructed, and you can insulate the viewing side as well when it needs protection from cold the most—during your sleeping hours, normally—by covering the front as well before you retire. Insulation will not only keep cold out but also will keep heat in if heat is generated from within the tank by a light or heater or anything else you use. Without insulation the glass sides of the tank will present practically no barrier to heat loss, and chilling can be fatal to the crabs. Insulation will reduce heat transfer dramatically, and if you live in a cold area and don't want to spend more than you have to to keep the crabs warm it will pay you to install insulation.

The insulation doesn't have to be anything fancy. A few slabs of styrofoam insulation material cut to fit will do the job nicely and probably will provide your neatest and least expensive treatment, but you can use anything that works. Putting insulation on the crab tank will make it more cumbersome and certainly won't improve the looks of your setup—in effect, you'll be the owner of a glass-fronted picnic cooler housing crawling crustaceans—but that's better than being an experimenter in crustacean cryogenics. Don't take the crabs' temperature requirements lightly; they *must* be kept warm to be kept living.

All in all, I think that the best way for you to keep the crabs warm when there's a significant danger that the room housing them will get too cold is to insulate the crabs' tank and use a light to generate heat. You can experiment with bulbs of different wattages to see which gives you a sufficient but non-broiling heat; in general it will be better to keep a fairly constant heat on the low side than to alternate periods of great heat followed by chill. In other words, keep a bulb of smaller wattage on for a long time, not a big bulb on for a short time. Don't worry about having the crabs disturbed by the light; they'll get used to it. Besides, you can use the light to provide warmth and still let your crabs get all the beauty sleep they need by providing shaded areas in the tank while the light is on. That way they'll have a choice about whether they want to be in the darker or lighter areas of the tank.

Before you can intelligently select the hermit crab meant for you, you'd better read this book first!

Selecting Your Crabs

Land hermit crabs of the genus *Coenobita* are fairly live-and-let-live animals as crustaceans go, so they can be housed in groups. In fact, they do better when kept in groups than when kept singly. They're also more fun to watch when they're kept in groups, so you should try to obtain more than one crab. How many you get will depend on the size of the crabs and the size of your tank—I'd say a fair rule of thumb to follow would be 1½ gallons of tank space per inch of crab. On that basis you could have three 1-inch crabs or one 3-inch crab in a 5-gallon tank, six one-inchers or two three-inchers in a 10-gallon tank. Tanks of longer and lower configuration than standard fish tanks would allow the keeping of more crabs, because they'd allow more floor space; taller, narrower tanks would allow less.

WHAT TO LOOK FOR

Choosing your crabs is no big complicated operation. You go down to your pet shop and pick out a few lively crabs, avoiding those that look sick or damaged (or dead). A damaged crab would be one that's obviously deformed or squashed up or in general down and out, but I couldn't tell you what a sick one looks like. I'm sure that if you saw a 3-inch worm hanging off a 2-inch crab or saw tiny little parasites crawling all over your potential purchase you'd steer clear of it, but in general it's hard to give you any standards to judge by. What you have to do is to exercise normal caution and go by the big tip-off that can be used with just about any type of animal that you're thinking of purchasing, whether it's a crab or a bird or a fish or a dog: inactivity. Stay away from any crab that remains comparatively immobile while its fellows are comparatively active. If most of the crabs in a dealer's crab tank are crawling or climbing around, while one or a few are remaining relatively motionless, make your pick from among the crawlers and climbers and let the stay-puts stay put.

Missing appendages would of course be a very sensible reason for passing up other types of pet animals, but with crabs missing appendages are of much lesser concern. The appendages can be regenerated, so don't make a big deal over a missing leg. That doesn't mean, though, that you should actively seek out crabs missing legs just so that you'll be able to witness the regeneration process; you'll be better off with a crab possessing a full complement of equipment. But if you have to make a choice between an inactive crab and one missing a leg or two, take the slightly maimed crab—it's a better investment. In land hermit crabs, chronic inactivity often precedes death.

THE SIZE OF THE CRABS YOU CHOOSE

Hermit crabs are not normally big bullies, so it's possible to house big ones with little ones. Yet it's not wise to let the differentials in your crabs' sizes be so great that one of them immediately assumes, by virtue of its greater bulk, the position of unchallenged champion. Such a crab could very easily become a bully in short order, so why take a chance? Putting a really big crab in among obvious underlings is tempting fate, because under the unnatural conditions you've created for your captives it might very well quickly learn to take advantage of its size to deprive its fellows of both food and tranquility. Besides, you just might be unlucky enough to obtain for yourself the crustacean equivalent of the Boston Strangler. Land hermit crabs of the genus *Coenobita* are not noted for their aggressiveness, but you have to figure that any crab in the same family as a certified whacker like Bad News Birgus, the coconut crab, has a pretty good homicidal streak in its family, so it's safer to play safe.

After you've kept crabs for a while you'll notice that smaller crabs are much more active and inquisitive—and therefore more fun to watch—if they're not forced into the presence of crabs much larger than themselves. The big boys put a damper on the smaller crabs' activities, even if they don't actually harm them.

If you're buying more than one crab, try to get crabs of roughly the same size. Small, big or medium as you choose, but they should all be about the same size. Don't be concerned about the sex of the crabs, however. Males and females can be told apart if you know what to look for, but looking for it entails removing the crabs from their shells. Removing a crab from its shell is not a safe (for the crab) operation, and since 1. males and females act alike anyway and 2. you have no chance at all of breeding the crabs, there is not much point in trying to sex them.

The crabs vary in price according to their size, with the biggest crabs commanding the highest prices. That in itself is a good reason for beginners to choose the smaller crabs, but there's also another: small shells cost less than large shells, so a big crab can cost you much more for providing alternative housings.

When you must buy your hermit crabs, get all the same species as some species are antagonistic to others. First, of course, examine them (left and right) to be sure they're healthy. Then observe them (below) as often as possible to be sure there is no combat!

THE SPECIES YOU CHOOSE

Every land hermit crab I've seen offered for sale in pet shops is of the species *Coenobita clypeatus*, the species that ranges from Florida to Venezuela and onto Caribbean islands. There are other species, some more colorful than *C. clypeatus*, but they're not currently being sold in quantity. Chances are great, then, that the species you obtain will also be *C. clypeatus*.

If it happens, though, that you're ever offered crabs of two different species, I'd be careful about keeping them together unless the seller/giver is able to assure you that they'll live together in peace. There might be natural antagonism between different species. At present there is very little chance that shops will offer a mixture of species, but that situation could change with the passage of time as people living in other treecrab-holding areas try to turn their crabs into a cash crop by selling them to dealers in pet livestock. I've never kept any species but *C. clypeatus*, so I've never been able to observe interactions among different species. The crabs probably get along together well enough, but you never can tell. You can be sure that one land hermit crab that won't live in harmony with its relatives is the coconut crab, a cannibalistic killer.

Your imagination can run away with you when setting up your tank. The Eiffel Tower replica, and other items which are painted or may contain lead, should be avoided as crabs have strong claws and they can easily loosen paint and eat it.

Setting Up
the
Crab
Tank

The ideal crab tank layout would be one that is easy and economical to set up and provides what the crabs need in an esthetically appealing-to-you motif. Let's divorce from our discussion the idea of my suggesting a layout that's esthetically appealing to you; I wouldn't even attempt it. That leaves us with economy and utility and ease of handling. From those three, let's drop economy; you already know or will soon find out what decorative items (coral, driftwood, shells, etc.) cost, and you'll be either willing or unwilling to spring for them. I wouldn't try to influence you one way or the other.

That leaves us with one topic, the meat of this discussion: what the crabs need. We've already talked about what they need in terms of heat and space and moisture, so let's see whether we can meld those things into the crab tank's layout, coming up at the same time with some practical suggestions for how to make things easy on yourself.

Assuming that you already have your tank and your lighting/heating equipment, you'll need only some sand or gravel and a few doodads for the tank. The substrate will be strictly utilitarian, but the doodads will be partly utilitarian and partly decorative. Let's take them in order.

THE BOTTOM COVERING

When you're setting up your crabarium you have a basic decision to make: should you cover the bottom of the tank with something, or should you leave it bare? Going strictly from the standpoint of which is easier for you, bare would be better, because leaving the bottom bare would make the tank much easier to maintain. Too bad that ease of maintenance isn't the only thing you have to consider. You have to consider the crabs' requirements, too, and the crabs don't like it bare. For one thing, a bare-bottom tank in which they have nothing but glass on which to put their legs makes for an overly slick surface on which to walk, and they're pretty maladroit to begin with. For another, it provides no cushion onto which they can safely fall when they—as they definitely will—push each other off the pieces of driftwood or tree branches or whatever else you provide for them to climb on. For yet another it offers absolutely no protection for a molting crab. A molting crab *has* to have something into which it can submerge its freshly molted soft body. If it can't hide, it's dead, and it can't hide if it has no bottom covering to dig into.

All in all, a bare tank is no good. The land hermit crab tank should have a bottom covering of some kind. That brings us to the consideration of this question: which type of bottom covering is best? Obviously you have a great number of bottom coverings to use. Sand, pebbles, gravel, crumpled newspapers, crushed glass, straw, wood ashes, soybeans, cherry pits, rusty nails, carrot tops and wine corks, not to mention cigaret filters and carpet fuzz, all come to mind. Of them all, sand and gravel are best. So the choice of bottom covering boils down to a choice between sand and gravel.

Wild land hermit crabs regularly bury themselves in damp sand. We assume that they do it partially to obtain protection (out of sight, out of mind) but partially also to keep their gills moist. They have to keep their gills moist, remember, or they'll die. They are accustomed, in other words, to sand. They like sand better than any other substrate in which to dig. Gravel is less good as a moisture preserver and offers much more resistance to the crabs' burrowing. Gravel, however, is for many crab owners much more easily obtained and more economical to use.

My opinion is that sand is the better substrate to use but that if you use gravel you won't be sacrificing much. I believe that although digging into damp sand may be the natural way for land hermit crabs to keep their gills moist, having a couple of inches of damp sand in the bottom of your crab tank is asking for trouble. Damp sand and food leftovers from the crabs make a bad combination; you can end up with a miniature Black Hole of Calcutta. Besides, you don't need to provide damp sand. You have available to you a highly unnatural but highly efficient and convenient method of keeping the crabs' gills moist: you can dunk the crabs. Once or twice a day, submerge the crabs in tepid water; that will give their gills all the moistness they need to function properly, and the crabs won't need to burrow into damp sand. Since a daily dunk will obviate the need for a damp substrate, you'll be able to use the much more convenient and easy to care for dry substrate in the form of dry sand or gravel. You can even use a combination of the two, keeping sand in a separate receptacle but surrounding that receptacle

Hermit crabs are scavengers. They will eat anything they find, from hard dog biscuits to a dead fish.

with gravel, letting the crabs make the choice of where they want to spend their time.

Dry sand or gravel is much easier to remove from the tank than damp sand, and you definitely should change the substrate occasionally, because land hermit crabs are cruddy little devils. What they don't eat they leave or, worse yet, bury. What they leave or bury stagnates; what stagnates stinks. If you're not careful your delightful little crabarium can become a miniature garbage dump. Your cover will help to keep the stench inside, but who needs it? The smell, unfortunately, is one of those insidious stinks that sneaks up on you. Because you're continually exposed to it, it grows on you gradually, and you're not really aware of it until some luckless visitor to your home gags and retches his way across your livingroom floor. So I'm telling you: use a substrate, but change it on a regular basis. If you can't change it, clean it. The best way to clean it is to boil it, skimming off what effluvium comes to the top, and then bake it. Boil it long and bake it hot. When you clean or discard the substrate, give the rest of the tank a thorough cleansing at the same time.

Pet shops and tropical fish specialty shops often sell finely granulated coral under the name "coral sand" for use in saltwater aquaria. This is about the best type of sand you can use for your crabs. It's expensive, though. Beach sand is good. It has the proper fineness, and people living near the ocean can obtain all the free beach sand they need. If you use beach sand, try to use sand from a permanently dry area above the high tide mark; sand from close to the water's edge might have too much organic (and potentially putrefying) matter in it. The builder's sand used in most cement work is too coarse, really more a fine gravel than a true sand. A very good approximation of beach sand (in fact it might just be glorified beach sand) is the sand sold for use in children's sandboxes. This stuff is usually starkly white and is cheap enough. Unfortunately, it comes in 50-pound and 100-pound sacks, which is much more than you'll need at any given time, so you have to store the excess unless you're willing to junk it. Unfortunately again, it's not always available, and you don't have any guarantee that you'll be able to lay hands on it.

Another sand that you can use is the sand used for creating sand "paintings," the craze of a few years ago. This sand comes in different colors and is available in much smaller packages. It's much more expensive than sandbox sand on a pound for pound basis, but it's still cheap enough, especially now that the sand painting fad has just about run its course. If you use sand-painting sand, be certain that it's color-fast.

THINGS TO CLIMB ON

Because land hermit crabs can climb and seem to enjoy climbing, and because watching them climb is fun, it makes sense for you to give them climbable items. Pieces of driftwood are excellent, but try to get smooth, barkless pieces. You don't want any cracks or fissures in the driftwood, because those cracks and fissures make handy places for the deposition of uneaten food. Land hermit crabs and driftwood are natural partners—the crabs even occasionally pick on and eat pieces of soft wood—but the crabs will climb on other things as well. Pieces of coral are great for climbing on, and the crabs love them. Unfortunately, pieces of coral also are great to drop uneaten food into, and they're very difficult to clean. Pieces of coral also are outrageously expensive.

ROCKS

Rocks make good decorations for land hermit crab tanks, and they can be useful as well. Slabs of rock can be arranged to provide shelter and shade, for example, and they can be used as bridges between places where the crabs are and where they want to go.

The most useful rocks are the slabs of shale (red or green, you can take your choice or mix and match) sold in pet shops for decorating fish tanks. But just about any rock will do;

You can decorate your hermit aquarium with many beautiful shells, even valuable shells if you are a collector. But how do you get your shell back from the crab? Put him in the cold for a short time until he becomes dormant, then simply pull him out of the shell. When he wakes up, have a new shell there for him. Always have water available for your crab (bottom facing page).

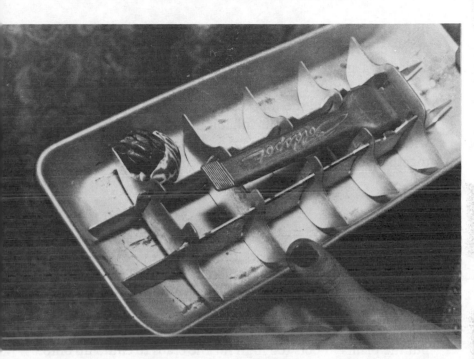

find what you like and use it. The only caution you have to observe in the use of rocks is that you avoid making any precarious balances. It won't do to have one slab balanced so gingerly on another that a slight shift in the base of the construction will send the topmost rock(s) crashing through the sides of the tank or onto its inhabitants. Once you're satisfied with a particular arrangement it might pay you to join it together semi-permanently with silicone cement or hot-melt glue.

PLANTS

Plants make very nice decorations for crab tanks—but not for long. The crabs eat them. Leaves, stalks, roots, everything. They even eat cactus plants. They pull the needles out to get at the flesh of the plant, and then they eat the flesh.

The best way to keep living plants in the crab tank is to put the plants in pots too high for the crabs to climb up onto. This method doesn't look good, but it's effective. Unmolested by the crabs, many plants will thrive in the bright, humid atmosphere of the tank. Another way to keep plants in the tank if you feel you have to is to partition the plants off from the crabs. Obtain a slab of glass that will fit lengthwise or back to front—or even diagonally, if that's what appeals to you—across the tank and cement it in place with silicone cement. Keep the crabs and their accoutrements in one area and the plants and their planting medium in the other. The glass doesn't have to be tall enough to reach the top of the tank, just high enough to prevent the crabs from getting into the plant area. If leaves from the plants overhang the glass and drip over into the crabs' quarters, no harm done (unless you're using poisonous plants); the crabs will just nibble them off.

If you're not a plant nut but still like the way plants can dress up the tank, you can use plastic plants. The crabs will eat wood but not plastic.

SHELLS

Empty shells have a specific role to play in a land hermit crab tank. They're more than just decorations. You should have plenty of empty shells in the tank. Go ahead and scatter them all over the place. If you keep them clean they can't do any harm. You'd be amazed to see how often the crabs will examine and re-examine the empty shells in the tank. They might never make a switch, but that won't stop them from examining the shells as if they were at least considering making a move—they'll go over the same shells time and time again. You'll be amused also to see the degree of thoroughness with which the shells are examined. The crabs don't just give a passing look and a cursory heft to the shells; they poke them and stroke them and turn them and twist them and stick their legs into them and even sometimes make tentative changeovers, getting their abdomens part of the way into a new shell before scurrying back into the old one. Let's face it; the crabs have a lot of time on their hands, so they might as well spend it in pondering the making of a potentially beneficial shell switch as in mindless pacing of the tank floor or digging themselves into a sand cocoon. It makes sense, then, for you to provide them with a good number and a good variety of shells, and you can always liven things up for the crabs by making occasional replacements. After one group of shells has been in the tank long enough to blunt even the crabs' seemingly inexhaustible enthusiasm for shell-shuffling, take out that group and replace it with a new one. The crabs' interest will be intensified by the arrival of "new" shells. They'll go into a frenzy of house-hunting, something that's always fun to watch. You don't have to be concerned that the crabs will get bored with the game. They don't realize that you're just shuffling around one shopworn group after another; their memories are not that good.

Incidentally, if you observe the crabs closely enough, you'll notice that a crab will often steadfastly reject a shell while it's lying around in his tank in one group, then eagerly

When selecting shells for your hermit crabs, don't
be impressed too much by the size of the shell.
Look at the size of the cavity into which the grow-
ing hermit crab must fit!

grab that same shell when you re-introduce it into the tank after having removed it for a week or two. There is no sensible-to-us reason for such action, because neither the shell nor the crab will have changed its physical properties in the intervening time—the crab can't grow, remember, until it molts, so it won't have become any larger—but they do it anyway.

Another thing you'll notice is that the crabs will examine more than just shells as potential coverings for their abdomens. Any small solid object having an aperture wide enough to let the crabs examine the object's interior will draw some interest from them. Tiny bottles, ends of metal tubing, thimbles, whatever—they all get a look-see. I've never seen a crab actually abandon a real shell for one of these objects, but I've seen them think enough of the phonies to get partway out of their shells before giving up.

Not all shells are equally suitable for use by the crabs. The size of the opening of a shell is of course important, but so is the shell's interior configuration. The crabs will seek out shells having internal whorls that more or less conform to the whorls into which the crabs will structure their abdomens, which is more or less circular, with the hindmost part tucked up into the foremost part. The shape of the opening to the shell is important also. The crabs feel most comfortable in shells in which they can block off the entrance by using their legs and claws, especially their bigger claw, as a stopper. Therefore they usually seek out shells that have roughly circular openings and avoid shells that have parabolic openings. You should use the crabs' preferences to take your clue about which shells you provide. Try to give them what they want and need. Pet shops that sell land hermit crabs often sell bags of empty shells that you can use as your basic stock of alternative housing units, and in some places you also can buy individual shells. If you live near the ocean, or if you live in an area that has land snails, you can of course pick up a bundle of free shells.

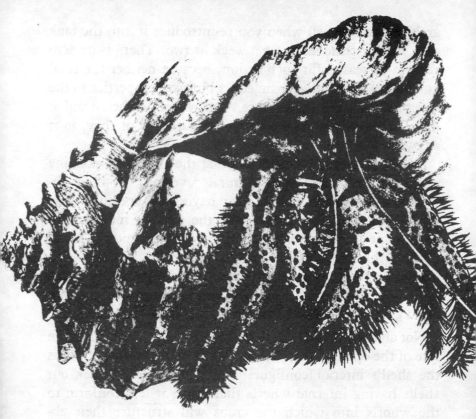

Feeding

Big crabs eat more than small crabs, of course. If you find a good pelleted food at your petshop, you can adjust how much you feed to the appetite of your pet.

Land hermit crabs eat practically anything, in any condition. They will eat both animal matter and vegetable matter, and they'll eat it just about any way it's served to them. Meats, fruits, cereals—they'll take them all. Considering that in the wild they are primarily scavengers and, to a lesser degree, minor predators, their nonspecialized tastes are to be expected. When you're a scavenger you get your bill of fare catch as catch can; you take what you can get or go hungry—and you often do exactly that, go hungry. Land hermit crabs are not concerned with their food's freshness either; where certain items are concerned, the deader the better.

The catholicity of land hermit crabs' tastes, however, doesn't mean that they don't have preferences. They generally go after meat-based foods more readily than they go after

plant-based foods. Whereas if you were to drop in a small piece of celery or apple the crabs would eventually get to it, meandering their way over the bottom of the tank until they come upon the food and start to eat it, a piece of meat dropped into the tank will have more of a tendency to get them moving to it. For the vegetables, in other words, they amble over; for the meat they drop what they're doing and head for it.

Working on the basis that land hermit crabs, even those that live comparatively far inland, are still tied to the sea, the best meats for your crabs would be the flesh of fish and shellfish. It can be cooked, but it doesn't have to be. One way for you to provide a steady supply of fish and shellfish is to keep a small piece frozen in the refrigerator or freezer and to cut off a tiny piece or two as needed. Frozen foods should be thawed out before they're given to the crabs, but you don't have to leave them standing around at room temperature to thaw out; to hasten the process, drop them into hot water. And when you remove the food from the water, don't remove any excess water that clings to the food. Feed the food wet; the extra wetness won't hurt, and it might help. Fish and shellfish have a value over and above the fact that they are probably the usual meats eaten by land hermit crabs in the wild. They also are the least greasy of all easily and economically available meats, and that's a big point in their favor. You definitely don't want to leave greasy foods hanging around in your crab tank.

Probably the most convenient, and no doubt among the best, foods to use for your land hermit crabs are the foods specifically formulated for feeding to the crabs. If processed by a reputable manufacturer, such a food will contain a number of different meat and vegetable substances, plus vitamins and minerals, supposedly useful to and assimilable by the crabs. You can usually get a line as to the utility of the food by examining the label on the food container; a good food will usually list a wide variety of ingredients and a high proportion of fish and shellfish meats in its constituents. Many foods designed for feeding tropical fish are fine for land hermit crabs as well. Additionally, they are available in many different forms (granules, pellets, flakes—even freeze-dried chunks), and you can select the form most convenient for you to use.

Your crabs will accept scraps from your table, and certain table scraps—fresh fruit and vegetables especially—should be provided on a regular basis.

One type of food that you can experiment with is live food, living insects and the like. The crabs catch and eat living insects in the wild, and there is no reason (apart from your squeamishness) why they can't eat them in captivity. If you reason that most insects that you're likely to capture and be able to feed to your crabs offer specific nutritional benefits to the crabs because of their possession of an exoskeleton made up mostly of the same material as the crabs' own exoskeleton, you may not be right, but you're not far off the track. In any event, you can have a lot of fun feeding living insects to the crabs. There is a nice sense of satisfaction to be derived from capturing a pesty fly or mosquito or whatever, pulling off its wings and a leg or two and dumping the rotten little pest into the lair of your waiting and appreciative crustacean executioners. It's basic justice, and it's fun to watch. On a more somber note: don't feed your crabs insects that have been exposed to insecticides.

HOW MUCH AND HOW OFTEN TO FEED

Land hermit crabs don't eat much. Big crabs eat more than small ones, naturally, but even big crabs eat surprisingly little. There is no hard and fast rule you can use to determine how much to feed a given number of crabs at a given time, so the best thing you can do is to be governed by experience based on your own observations of your own crabs. Give the crabs time to find and examine the proffered tidbit, then see how much of it they consume. Give them all they'll clean up

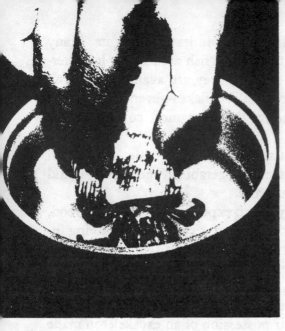

You should equip your crab tank with a water container in which the crabs can crawl and wet their gills. If kept without water they dehydrate and hang limp (right) when you hold them. They usually die when they dry out.

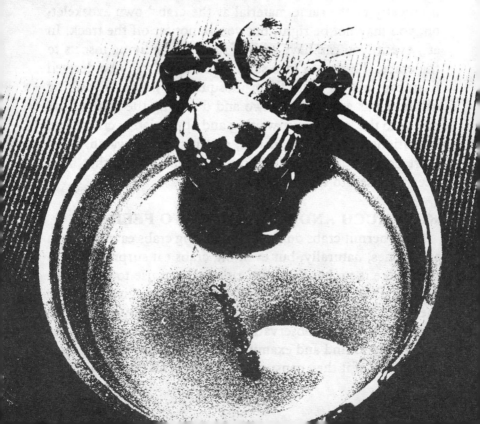

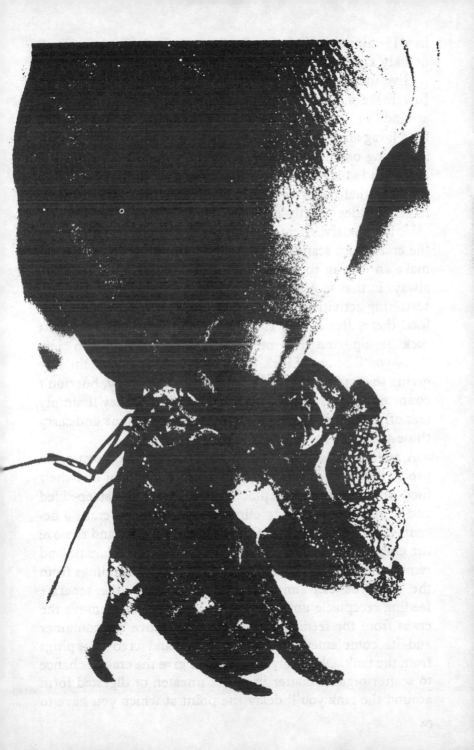

in a 15-minute period after finding the food; if they eat it all quickly and seem to be waiting for more, give them more.

Give them as much as they'll eat as often as they'll eat it. Just make sure that you don't confuse "eat" with "drag around" or "maul" or "hang onto." You don't want uneaten food lying around to rot in the tank; you don't want the crabs scattering or burying uneaten pieces around and under the gravel and sand; you don't want to let the crabs con you into thinking that they're eating what you're giving them when in reality they're only playing with it.

Unfortunately, there is not much you can do to prevent the crabs from scattering some food around the tank. If you make an area in the tank bare of gravel and place the food always in that spot, you'll be able to cut down on their food-scattering activities if they cooperate with you by eating the food there. But if they carry it away from where they first pick it up—and it's often their tendency to do just that—you'll be out of luck. You can try to fox them a little by giving them pieces of food too large to carry away, but don't count on that to solve the problem entirely; they'll simply tear off small pieces from the unmanageable chunk and carry those pieces away.

A method guaranteed to reduce the crabs' food-scattering proclivities to a minimum is to place both them and their food into a separate receptacle too deep, or too steep-sided and slippery, for them to climb out of, give the crabs a decent length of time to eat if they're of a mind to, and remove the crabs after that. If you want to play hygiene fanatic and remove both the uneaten food and the crabs' droppings from the tank you can simply leave the crabs in the separate feeding receptacle until they've evacuated; then remove the crabs from the feeding container and remove the container and its complement of uneaten food and crab droppings from the tank. Obviously if you never give the crabs a chance to scatter organic matter in either uneaten or digested form around the tank you'll delay the point at which you have to reset the tank entirely because it's starting to get gamy. But I think that that's pushing things much too far. It's better to let the crabs mess up their tank and force you into a complete overhaul once in a while than to go through all the rigmarole you'd have to go through to prevent the natural consequences of their ways. My advice: let them slop it up all they want—but make sure that you break down and clean the tank thoroughly at regular intervals. I also advise that when you give the tank an overhaul you junk all of the sand and gravel in it instead of trying to save a few cents. Replace the sand and gravel with fresh material.

THE WATER BOWL

Land hermit crabs don't drink in the same way that we or the domestic animals that we're most familiar with drink. They don't stick their faces into water and lap it up. But they should be provided with water nonetheless. A bowl of water, for one thing, helps to provide humidity in the tank. For another, it provides a source of wetness in which the crabs can immerse themselves and be absolutely guaranteed of having a mechanism for keeping their gills moist.

You should equip your crab tank with a water container into which the crabs can crawl if they feel like it. And out of which they can crawl when they feel like it, of course. The container can be as decoratively unobtrusive as you like or as glaringly out of place as you like; that's up to you. For decorative nicety you can sink a shallow receptacle into the gravel, more or less flush with the level of the gravel, and let the crabs wander in and out at will. You also could use an ashtray or plastic box or maybe the bottom of a #10 can of lima beans. What the water pool looks like doesn't matter to the crabs, and if it doesn't matter to you it shouldn't matter to anyone else. What does matter is that your water container be 1.) available to the crabs (they can climb in and out) and 2.) kept clean (they should not contract typhus from bathing in it).

The most common hermit crab found in most petshops is the *Coenobita* shown above and top, right. Lots of crabs are to be found throughout the tropical world both in freshwater and marine environments. The black crab shown on the bottom of the facing page was found on Eniwetok Island, one of the South Pacific islands which forms the Marshall Island group. This land crab should not be kept with *Coenobita* as it will probably tear it to shreds and eat it! Photo of *Birgus latro*, the black crab, by Scott Johnson. The common hermit, top facing page, was photographed by Ken Lucas.

If the crab outgrows the shell in which it "lives" and it cannot find another shell (top), then it will dig into the sand (below) and attempt to protect its abdomen in this manner. Photos by Kyn Tolson.

The first requirement is met easily enough by providing the container, if it's a deep one, with bridges in and bridges out or by keeping it shallow in the first place. The second is handled by changing the water frequently, frequently being defined as at least once a day. The water that goes into the pool should be about 80° F.

It doesn't matter much whether you use salt or fresh water. If you want to use salt water in the form of artificial sea water you can purchase a seawater mix at the pet shop where you purchase the crabs; the mixes come with full directions for mixing. It wouldn't cost very much to mix up five or ten gallons of artificial sea water using one of the mixes, and those five or ten gallons would last you for a long, long time, but you don't need salt water for the crabs.

If you notice that your crabs like to drag their food over to the water container and dunk their pieces of it into the water before eating, don't interfere. It may be a little sloppy, but it won't hurt anything. I've seen some crabs that had developed the habit of eating only after they had positioned themselves in the water dish; they wouldn't eat anywhere else. I have no idea of the significance of their actions, but I left them alone. Since the water receptacle had to be cleaned and replenished on a daily basis anyway, their messing around with food in the water didn't hurt anything.

Learn how to hold a hermit crab. Don't squeeze it.

Handling Land Hermit Crabs

Hermit crabs do not like to be handled. In nature only an enemy would touch them. To show their displeasure, they often "clam up" sealing their home with their huge claw. This claw can give you a nasty bite, too. Be careful.

From the standpoint of the benefit of the crabs, they should be handled as infrequently as possible. They don't like being handled. They show their dislike by either withdrawing as far as possible into their shells, sealing off the entrance by using their large claw as a plug, or by reaching out as far as they can and trying to nip the offending fingers of the handler. Usually they don't do this until they've gone through their withdrawal routine, but sometimes they do it right after being picked up.

My experience is that you should handle your crabs as little as possible. Handling them is dangerous. It's dangerous to the handler, and it's dangerous to the crabs. It's dangerous to the handler because a nip from a good-size crab hurts; if a 3-inch or 4-inch crab were to nip you on a fleshy part of the hand (the nice meaty part at the base of the thumb, for instance) you wouldn't forget it in a hurry. You especially wouldn't forget it in a hurry if the crab, after taking its nip, hung on for a while, as they've been known to do. I don't know what type of musculature powers a big land hermit crab's big claw, but it's powerful. A talented and well-trained crab could be put into service as a pair of vise-grip pliers.

That's why handling crabs is dangerous to them. The natural immediate reaction of someone nipped by a crab is to try to shake the nipper off. The movement is almost reflexive, like squinting an eye that has something in it. In order to refrain from doing it you have to make a conscious effort of will to keep from shaking off, and thereby possibly killing, the crab. That's where the danger lies: the nip leads to a reflexive shake and jerk that in turn lead almost always to an automatic cracking of crab against wall or floor or table. Just dropping a crab onto a hard surface can kill it, so you can picture what *propelling* it against that surface will do. The bigger the crab, the bigger the danger.

There is not much to be gained from handling the crabs anyway, so why do it? They are not the kind of animals you pick up and pet and coo at, so there's not much point in trying to get cuddly with them. If you want something to pet, get a puppy or kitten. Land hermit crabs are for watching, not stroking.

That's not to say that you should fear them and avoid handling them entirely. When you need to pick them up—for tank cleaning or examination or any other sensible purpose—go ahead and pick them up. If you do it right neither you nor the crabs will be hurt. The right way to pick up a crab is to grasp it firmly at the rear of its shell, far enough back that it can't reach you with either of its front claws. What you want to avoid is constant needless handling. Don't let visitors to your home handle the crabs, even if they say that they know what they're doing. I'm not talking only about visiting children here, either. I'm including adults. The kids may be more persistent in their hounding to be allowed to handle the crabs and probably will engage in much more clandestine crab-clutching than an adult would, but the adult pests can be bad enough in their own way.

Although it's true that the crabs will become used to handling if you handle them enough and can become "tame" to the point of not pinching you if you allow them to wander over your hand or arm, your best course of action is to leave them pretty much alone. There is simply nothing to be gained by picking them up and playing with them. But if you insist on handling them, choose the smallest crabs to carry on your love affairs with. They're less of a danger to you, and you're therefore less of a danger to them.

Another point that you might want to consider as a reason for not handling your crabs more than is necessary is that not all crabs respond to handling the same way. Some become more docile, but some become more cantankerous. Some individuals become accustomed to being picked up and pawed at, to the degree that they become resigned enough not to give any evidence of obvious resentment. Others, though, react just the opposite. Although they don't make any attempt to nip the first few times they're handled, they grow progressively more feisty with each succeeding pick-up. In other words, some crabs are not nippers to begin with but become nippers from being handled.

Having said all of the above, I know full well that you're going to ignore it. You're going to have a natural inclination to want to play with the crabs by putting them into action on your livingroom floor or kitchen table or someplace else. For all I know you're already making plans to put them into the

There are many ways to house your hermit crab. The best is in an aquarium which has been sealed at the top both to keep the crabs in and enemies out! When you add too many ornaments (top facing page), it makes cleaning more of a chore. A neat little setup is sufficient (bottom facing page). In any case, before adding your crab to the tank (above), be sure you have larger shells into which the crab can grow.

A LIST OF DON'TS!

1. Don't throw crabs around. Even though they are hard, they are still fragile
. . . like glass. Don't thrust them at people! 2. Don't let your crab out of sight. If
he crawls around on the floor he might be stepped on or mangled by another
animal. Or, your cat might get a nipped nose! 3. Don't put crabs on a lofty perch
from which they might crawl off and crash to their doom. 4. Protect your crabs
from other animals; which also means protect your animals from the crab, too.

bathtub to play submarine or maybe glue sticks to them and make believe they're jelly apples. Maybe you'll put small ones in icecubes and drop them into guests' drinks. That's up to you. If you're going to do anything like that, though, I'd like to give you a few sensible ground rules to make things safer for you and the crabs.

1.) Don't thrust crabs at people. Visitors to your home—members of your own family, for that matter—won't relish the notion of having you springing out of nowhere and trying to jam a crab up their nose. This is a plainly stupid stunt that just might earn you a few loose teeth.

2.) Don't lose sight of the played-with crab. If you have to mess around by letting a crab or crabs crawl around on the floor, okay—but keep your eyes on them if you do. A minute or two of inattention can lose a crab permanently.

3.) Don't put crabs on raised surfaces and leave them there unattended. The crabs don't have the sense not to creep off elevated surfaces. Coming right to the edge of a tabletop, they'll often keep right on going instead of backing off. They therefore fall off and crack themselves hard, perhaps beyond repair. Remember the Humpty Dumpty motto: having a great fall doesn't mean you'll have a good winter.

4.) Don't let other animals get to your crabs. It might be ten thousand potential yuks to throw a big crab in front of the family dog and watch the action, but it's dangerous to both crab and dog/cat/ferret/whatever. A big crab just might fasten itself to some sensitive part of an unsuspecting pet animal's anatomy, and that would be bad. Or that animal could just sit back and wait for an unsuspecting crab to start walking away and then POUNCE!, resulting in one dead crab. Land hermit crab vs. other pet encounters usually end in a standoff, with neither animal being much interested in the other, but they *can* be dangerous.

Land Hermit Crab Behavior

The crab above has just outgrown its
shell. It lines up the new shell and explores it before
moving into it (facing page).

You'd better not expect too much from your land hermit crabs by way of sparkling behavior, because you're not going to get it. They're plodders, and they're not very bright. In fact, going by the standards that we normally use to judge the comparative intelligence of animals, they're downright stupid. If you want to take the position that it's not—because of the great physiological differences—fair to judge land hermit crabs' intelligence by testing their reactions in a particular situation and comparing those reactions against what a dog or pig or mouse would have done if faced with the same set of circumstances, okay. I have no axe to grind either way. I find land hermit crabs interesting, so I don't really care whether they're regarded as relatively intelligent or absolutely dull-witted. My experiences with them, though, force me to say that they're not very swift.

Take the matter of avoiding obstacles as a case in point. Land hermit crabs don't avoid obstacles in their path. They climb over them. Sometimes easily, sometimes clumsily, sometimes fast, sometimes agonizingly slowly—but almost always unnecessarily. Looking at them pull one of their anything-in-my-path-gets-climbed-over routines practically forces you to scream, "Walk around it, stupid! Walk around!" But they don't walk around; they walk over. If you're charmed by displays of pure mulishness, be prepared to be charmed by land hermit crabs. What it is is just a 100% lack of what you and I would regard as plain common sense: the crabs don't have it. Maybe they're showing us a better way to do things; maybe they're exhibiting contempt for our way of thinking; maybe they're just having fun. I don't know, but it bugs me to see a bigger ambulatory animal show less smarts than a cockroach.

Yet in certain ways the crabs are clever dogs. Escaping, for example, is a specialty of theirs. They show as much ingenuity in escaping from an enclosure that you've designed to hold them as they show dumbness in avoiding obstacles. I once watched one of my larger crabs climb straight up a thin piece of plastic that I had temporarily propped up in a corner of the tank. (It usually served as a divider between a gravel area and a sand area.) I don't mean that the piece of plastic—about two inches wide and an eighth of an inch thick—was *inclined* in the corner; it was straight up in the corner, flush against the glass, 90° to the bottom of the tank. The crab, though, must not have understood that it shouldn't have been able to ascend a purely vertical smooth surface and went merrily straight up like a commando scaling a rope. It just kept advancing itself bit by bit by gripping the edges of the plastic with its big and little gripping claws, one claw to each edge, and hauling itself upward. Very purposeful, very methodical, assuming that 1. the crab wanted to escape and 2. that it recognized the piece of plastic as a way out. It seems, though, that the crabs will exercise brainpower only in the pursuit of forbidden objectives. If you actively wish them well in doing the sensible thing—if you *want* them to show some cleverness, in other words—they'll only muddle along like so many ambulatory rocks.

CRAB MEETS CRAB

I mentioned before that it's wise policy not to mix crabs differing greatly in size, on the basis that you don't want to get the little ones killed. Cannibalism among pet land hermit crabs definitely is known to have occurred. Cases of one crab's being eaten by another, or by a group of others, *usually* have been the result of the recent molting of the eatees, but other instances have been reported. In such cases the eaters manage to get their victims out of their shells, and once out of its shell the potential victim is a goner. I don't know exactly how the Albert Fish types manage to accomplish the shell-shucking—I've never seen one land hermit crab force another out of its shell—but they do it. Probably they use roughly the same method as marine hermit crabs use, basically a system of knocks and raps and bashes and gouges, coupled with some spirited pulling and dragging. Marine hermit crabs don't, you should know, occupy only empty shells. Sometimes they roughhouse another hermit crab and take its shell. Among land hermit crabs, forcible eviction is performed, I believe, less for the purpose of getting a new shell than for the purpose of getting something good to eat. It might be done out of pure meanness or as punishment for transgression of some unknown-to-us hermit crab criminal code, for all we know. In any event, it's occasionally done, and the only way you can be completely certain of avoiding it is to keep the crabs separated. That's not really practical, so the next best thing you can do to avoid internecine mayhem is to group your crabs by size.

INDIVIDUALISM

Let me point out something here that most people don't pay enough attention to. It's this: pet land hermit crabs dif-

Hermit crabs are not fussy pets. Their requirements are simple but definite. They easily freeze to death since they are tropical animals. They must eat and have water to keep their gills wet. They must be protected from injuring themselves as well as prevented from attacking other animals. An old aquarium (facing page) properly set up can be a living decoration as well as a hobby.

fer in behavior from individual to individual. Maybe they're not supposed to be different from one another, but they are. Some are bolder and more aggressive, some are shy and retiring, some are very active while others are sluggish, some seem to be relatively smarter and others relatively duller, and some are strictly psycho. They differ in food preferences and their liking for water and the degree of tenacity with which they hold onto their shells and in all kinds of other things as well. But in most cases you won't be able to observe those differences unless you maintain crabs that are roughly of the same size. A big size difference among the crabs is a big dampener of social interplay. A small crab, for instance, that might be a very active, amusing performer if maintained with crabs of its own size will usually turn into a do-nothing deadhead if kept among much bigger specimens. Look at it this way: how much fun would you be if you ran into King Kong every time you walked down the street?

I don't mean to imply that you can keep your crabs in a permanent party mood just by weeding out dwarfs and giants—some crabs will be zeroes no matter what you do to help their social life along—but in general you won't be able to get the most from your crabs unless you separate them by size.

MOLTING CRABS

Molting crabs deserve special attention. In the first place, the molting process is fascinating to observe, so if you have a potential shedder on your hands you should coddle it. Give it the extra attention it needs and you'll be well rewarded; don't give it that attention and it will be dead.

Molting crabs need moisture and security. A crab can't molt if it's deprived of moisture, because in crabs the molting process is accomplished primarily through hydrostatic pressure; a crab needs to build up enough "water pressure" in its body to split the old shell, pretty much the same way a weed builds up enough pressure in its cells to burst through concrete. And a molting crab needs security—by which I mean, essentially, isolation—because if it's not kept away from potential predators while it's in its freshly molted softshell stage it's doomed. Its enemies will pick it to pieces, because a freshly molted crab is practically defenseless. That's why it digs into the sand and keeps out of view until its armor has hardened up. And that's why as soon as it's hard-shelled again it beats it out of the sand and tries to get itself a good portable shield onto its backside.

So there are the two prime rules for the treatment of about-to-molt crabs: give them plenty of moisture, and keep them separated from their cannibalistic brethren. Lacking the possibility of keeping them separated, do the next best thing: don't crowd the crabs. Give them plenty of room. The more crowded they are the more dangerous they become to one another. The more room they have to themselves the less likely they are to kill one another. The third rule would be this: provide plenty of potential new shells to the newly molted crabs. They'll make a comical project out of picking out a new shell, and you'll enjoy watching them.

Unfortunately, there is no sure sign by which you can tell whether a crab is about to molt. Therefore there is no sure method by which you can separate potential molters from non-molters in advance if you keep a number of crabs together. You have to keep an eye out to see whether a crab has left its shell and buried itself in the sand; then move it to private quarters. You do, however, have a few guidelines to go by in picking out potential molters. Inactivity is one and not eating is another. They're not sure tip-offs—and they're no tip-offs at all to anyone who hasn't observed his crabs closely enough to notice individual differences among them—but at least they're something. Inactivity among the crabs is of course not a very abnormal state of affairs to begin with. It's not unusual for a crab to stay huddled up in a corner for many hours at a time, for instance. But if a relatively active, actively feeding crab rather suddenly becomes inactive and

The marine hermit crab above lives in the tropical oceans. Its scientific name is *Calcinus elegans*. Photo by Scott Johnson. On the facing page is another beautiful marine hermit crab, *Carcinus seurati*, living in a *Cymatium gemnatum* shell. Photo by Scott Johnson.

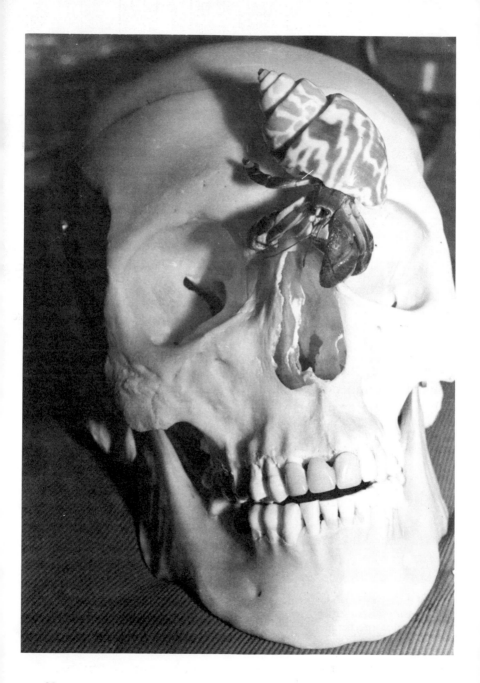

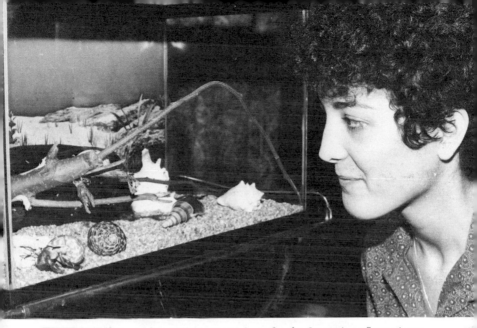

The skull (facing page) is available at petshops for the decoration of aquariums. It makes an interesting decoration for a hermit crab tank. Your hermit home should be enjoyed by everyone (above). They are ideal for doctors' and dentists' offices.

doesn't eat, there's a possibility that its changed behavior signals an impending molt. If you run into a situation like that, isolate the oddly behaving crab. Even if nothing happens, you haven't lost anything but a little extra effort on your part.

BREEDING LAND HERMIT CRABS

Forget about breeding your crabs. Land hermit crabs place their eggs into the ocean for hatching, and when the eggs hatch the infant crabs (which don't look anything like adult hermit crabs) become part of the zooplankton of the ocean. They drift around eating and changing in structure until they're ready to change into normal land hermit crab appearance and begin their life on land. You couldn't replicate or even halfway simulate the conditions they require in their ocean-going state without going to an enormous effort and expense, so don't try. Save yourself money and frustration.

Diseases
and
Ailments

Roger Steene, one of the world's finest underwater photographers, caught this rare marine hermit crab, *Aniculus strigatus*. The cone shell home suits this flat species very well, but it does not live in shallow water too well and died shortly after capture because its requirements for depth and low light could not be met. The hermit home on the facing page is in the direct sun. With the top sealed on the tank, it cooked the poor hermit crab.

Very little is known about diseases and ailments in captive land hermit crabs. Not much more (maybe less) is known about diseases and ailments in wild land hermit crabs. Certainly the crabs have their parasites; just about everything else does, so why should land hermit crabs be an exception? And no doubt they have their circulatory and digestive and respiratory disorders, each of which will be recognized and named and prescribed for as land hermit crabs become more economically important. Right now, though, all of their ills boil down to the mysterious croak; the crab is outwardly well one day, dead the next.

It may be that the here today, gone tomorrow crabs were suffering all along from some malady that cried out for correction but went unsuspected and untreated because we don't recognize differences in appearance between healthy and sick crabs. No doubt some deaths are attributable to chronic ailments falling into this category. I think, however, that most deaths among captive land hermit crabs occur as the result of a continuous desiccation of the crabs. The crabs MUST have water. Now I know it might seem as if I'm beating a dead horse here by harping on something that should be just about self-evident to anyone who keeps a captive animal of any sort, but you'd be surprised at the number of land hermit crab owners who don't seem to make any connection between the fact that crabs are animals and that animals of all types distinctly depend on water to be able to live. They try to keep the crabs in a bone-dry environment, and you just can't get away with that. The crabs can't take it. Make it a regular practice to dunk your crabs in warm water once a day. Take them and place them right into the water bowl; then let them crawl out. If you don't have a water bowl permanently established in the tank, dunk them somewhere else. But dunk them at least once daily. A full dunking assures you that the crabs have been exposed to water and that their gills have been moistened. Don't worry that the crabs will drown; they may look as if they should never be put into water, but it won't hurt them. They can stay submerged much, much longer than you'd think without having any harm come to them. Often you'll notice that a crab won't move at all for minutes on end after you've completely submerged it in the water bowl, but the immersion won't hurt it; it will move out when it's ready. Make sure, however, that you give submerged crabs a chance to creep out of the bowl; they can stay submerged for a long time, but if they can't get out of the water eventually they'll drown. Either remove them from the bowl yourself or leave some type of bridge in the bowl upon which they can crawl their way out. They might not use the bridge (they like to do things the hard way by scrambling around the bottom of the bowl looking for every way out but the obvious one) if the sides of the bowl are low enough to let them hook a leg over the side and haul themselves out, but there is no harm in having it there.

Crabs on the way out flash one big danger signal: they don't fully retract into their shells when agitated. Poke a normal land hermit crab and he'll bottle himself up in his shell; poke a potential croaker and he'll make only a half-hearted, maybe quarter-hearted, effort to retreat into his refuge. The about-to-die crab just doesn't have the energy; he doesn't care anymore. Once a crab reaches this state there is nothing you can do for it; it's gone.

Dying crabs usually relax their grip on their shells. They extend their foreparts farther and farther from the shell and sometimes even leave the shell entirely. A dead crab, very unlike a healthy live one, is easy to remove from its shell. Just grip the cephalothorax and pull gently. The crab will come out with no trouble. If you want to use the shell again, scald it before adding it to your collection of backup housings. The scalding will kill whatever disease organisms or parasites might be living inside the shell.

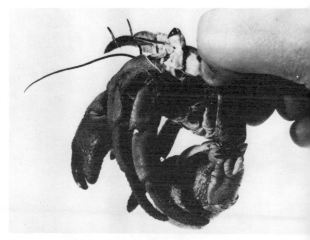

Dying crabs relax their grip on their shells.

HERMIT CRABS